PERVASIVE AGILITY AND AGILE FIRES IN SUPPORT OF DECISIVE ACTION

"In the 21st century, we do not have the luxury of deciding which challenges to prepare for and which to ignore."[1]
--President Barack Obama

From piracy to peacekeeping, from counterinsurgency to cybercrime, from humanitarian assistance to high intensity conflict—the United States Army must be prepared to confront any challenge on behalf of the nation. Unrelenting struggle among state and non-state actors across the full spectrum of conflict and played out within the context of a near real time global communication network and with exponential effects ricocheting and echoing through the hyper-connected global economy will be the new normal. The fluidity of the international system and the omnipresent threat of weapons of mass destruction sets conditions of enormous stakes; we must be prepared to respond to any emergency, either overseas or domestically, immediately—not six months from now, but now. A quick survey of major events and crises which have jockeyed for the attention of our national leaders over the last two years demonstrates the point that there is no obvious flashpoint on which to focus. We have witnessed a seemingly quickening succession of crises and evolving security predicaments: from the lingering messiness and instability of the various uprisings of the Arab spring (Tunisia, Egypt, Libya, Syria) to the evolving nuclear crisis and political standoff in Iran; from the death of Kim Jong-Il and an uncertain transition of power in the nuclear capable isolated regime of North Korea to the emergence of China as an economic powerhouse, a potential peer competitor, and a suspected sponsor of international cyber-attacks; from the narco-terrorism and criminal violence in Mexico, to failing and failed states in Africa. And with the knowledge that all of these crises are playing out against the enduring

1

backdrop of the unresolved war against Islamic extremism and international terrorism. If there is anything certain in the years ahead, it is uncertainty; any assertion to the contrary is a dangerous illusion.

We not only confront strategic complexity and uncertainty, but the difficulty of solving this Gordian knot is further compounded by a simultaneous problem of economic turmoil and fiscal uncertainty. To complicate matters, the nation faces fiscal and budgetary challenges as our national leaders come to grips with an ongoing global economic crisis. Ten years of wartime expenditures, Bush-era tax cuts, unforeseen recessions, persistent unemployment, soaring fuel prices, the collapse of the housing market, and a near breakdown of our financial system have all contributed to ballooning Government budget deficits. There is no simple way out of this dilemma; indeed, the dual problems of a stalled economy and runaway deficits may be locking the nation into a self-defeating spiral. Our national leaders are faced with the challenge of reducing deficits by cutting spending and raising revenues while simultaneously stimulating the arrested economy.[2] Internationally, the widespread, precarious debt crisis of our allies in Europe compounds and complicates our deep-seated economic challenges. Acknowledging the challenging and problematic economic environment that serves as the backdrop to our strategic imperative, President Barack Obama wrote that in order to meet our strategic defense challenges, "We must put our fiscal house in order here at home and renew our long-term economic strength."[3] Coupled with the strategic uncertainty of a dangerous world, the nation and the Army face a period of austerity, diminishing resources, and hard choices.

Simultaneously, the Army is undergoing a separate strategic transition that will challenge its leaders on its own terms, the foreseeable end of Counter-Insurgency operations in both Iraq and Afghanistan. With the withdrawal of forces from Iraq complete, and the near-term transition of our operations to our partners in Afghanistan, we will soon have a force that will execute the Army Force Generation Process (ARFORGEN) without the certainty of a Deployment Order, falling into a Contingency Expeditionary Force pool (CEF) with the possibility to deploy anywhere and do anything.

But in the midst of this perfect storm, a kaleidoscopic atmosphere of ambiguity, and complexity, there is one thing that is certain: we cannot allow doubt to disorient us and paralyze us; we cannot afford to remain idled while we wait for the next challenge to resolve and present itself in high definition.

In December 2009, General Martin Dempsey, serving at the time as the commander of the US Army's Training and Doctrine Command (TRADOC) anticipated this period of strategic uncertainty and transition that was just over the horizon and visualized the qualities necessary in the Army to meet the challenges of this transition. He wrote: "Ideas matter . . . ideas can serve as the driving force behind significant institutional change."[4] The fundamental idea he was referring to was the central concept of agility, supported by the underlying tenets of adaptability, versatility, and flexibility. Today, just two short years later, the strategic conditions that he envisioned are upon us, and General Dempsey, now the chairman of the Joint Chiefs of Staff, is attempting to actualize his vision and shape the US Joint Force into an agile and adaptable organization.

Our nation's senior leaders echo General Dempsey's assessment of the environment and the imperatives it imposes our nation's department of defense. Indeed, as President Barack Obama wrote in the Strategic Planning Priorities released in January 2012, "As we end today's wars and reshape our Armed Forces, we will ensure that our military is agile, flexible, and ready for the full range of contingencies." [5] Secretary of Defense Leon Panetta concurred with the President, writing, "We are shaping a joint force that will be smaller and leaner, but will be agile, flexible, ready, and technologically advanced."[6] Agility and adaptability are powerful ideas, and after surveying the ambiguous international environment where our next threat is impossible to predict, our senior leaders recognize the importance of these ideas. In describing the qualities of the force needed to confront these challenges, the concept of agility stands out as a strategic imperative.

You don't have to read between the lines. In this new age of complexity, uncertainty, and existential danger, adaptability and agility are specified capabilities. But this fundamental idea of agility raises questions: Can we adequately define agility within the context of the current strategic debate to achieve a common working understanding of agility and its component attributes that meets the intent of our senior leaders? Can we draw lessons learned from our recent operational experiences to guide future leaders in their quest for agility? In practical terms, can we create an effective blueprint or roadmap to guide future leaders in their pursuit of agility?

This paper will propose to answer these questions. First, this paper will develop a working definition of agility and its components by conducting a close reading of the concept of agility as it has evolved within our operational doctrine. Second, this paper will closely examine the concept of agility within the context of our most recent operational deployments over the last ten years in order to infer what agility in the future should look like. Finally, this paper will propose a practical roadmap to improved agility. Throughout this paper, we will closely examine the demands of agility on the fires warfighting function, one of the six nested doctrinal functions performed by Army forces in the context of our emerging doctrine of unified land operations. This paper will focus on the fires warfighting function as a case study for two reasons: first, to allow a more specific analysis of agility by focusing on Soldiers, leaders, and units tasked to perform a specific function within the umbrella concept of unified land operations; second, because the counter-insurgency (COIN) campaigns of the last decade arguably placed greater demands on the agility of the fires warfighting function and artillerymen than Soldiers, leaders or units of other branches or warfighting functions, and therefore, make them ideal subjects for analysis under the lens of agility. By answering these questions, this paper will attempt to contextualize the concept of agility as the appropriate evolution of doctrine in response to an uncertain and dangerous world, as well as to provide a commonly understood definition of agility, to foster a more complete understanding of the advantages and imperatives of agility (and adversely, the strategic risks associated with failing to achieve agility), and most importantly, to simplify the pursuit of agility for current and future Army leaders.

Section 1. Agility in the Abstract—Defining Agility

"You see a lot of guards in today's game who shoot when they should pass and pass when they should shoot; their games don't make sense."[7]
--Jeff Van Gundy, Former NBA coach

"Do I contradict myself? Very well then I contradict myself. (I am large, I contain multitudes.)"[8]
--Walt Whitman, *Song of Myself*

Agility as a concept is expansive and elastic enough to not only describe a point guard skillfully navigating through a zone defense towards the basket, but also a poet artfully deploying language, breathing vitality into words to manifest the spectrum of the human experience and condition. Agility is a large term; it contains multitudes. But that is cold comfort to an Army leader as he or she attempts to translate an abstraction, the ideal of agility, into concrete action—a specified task from the national command authority—while simultaneously dealing with the very real distractors of limited resources, finite training time, and competing priorities. Let's not beg the question; what does agility mean exactly? Can we isolate agility as a concept, agree on a common working definition, and identify subordinate components of agility that will be useful, practical, to current Army leaders? In order to arrive at this comprehensive definition, we will need to examine the commonly understood definition of agility in its everyday usage, account for the specialized components of agility as it has been used over the years in military doctrine, and examine agility in its context within the current strategic debate.

The dictionary is the obvious point of departure, a necessary and useful starting point. *Merriam Webster's collegiate dictionary* defines agility as:

"Marked by a ready ability to move with quick easy grace; having a quick, resourceful, and adaptable character; nimbleness, dexterity."[9]

While all of these definitional components of agility, these subordinate attributes, are undeniably positive, advantageous, and desirable, it's hard to envision building a training plan for an infantry platoon, or a forward support company, or a field artillery battalion that is assembled upon this shallow semantic foundation. When the President and the Secretary of Defense cited agility as an imperative in the *National Defense Priorities*, it is highly unlikely that they were calling for the Department of Defense to invest extensively in obstacle courses across our installations and bases, so that our forces can hone their ability to move quickly and nimbly, adapting to physical obstacles with grace and dexterity.

It is safe to say that the concept of agility that our senior leaders are calling for means more than the simple dictionary definition. Addressing this need to achieve a common understanding of agility as a fundamental concept for complex organizations, David Alberts, the current director of research for the assistant secretary of defense for Networks and Information Integration (OASD NII), wrote, "Over the years, there has been some discussion of agility—its definition, its constituent properties, its attributes, and its measurement. Many of the words used to describe agility are understood a bit differently in different communities." While we have had problems achieving a common understanding of the concept in the past, Alberts goes on to argue that it is worth the effort to keep trying. He states, "The investment in semantic interoperability is worthwhile because an in-depth understanding of agility is required to transform the way we think, the investments we make, and the way we measure value."[10]

With the dictionary definition as a starting point, perhaps the best approach to a more comprehensive working definition of agility is through its appearance in military and operational doctrine. Published doctrine holds an important place in the Army's canon. As John Nagl, a former US Army Armor officer and noted commentator on Army operations wrote in his widely-read critique of the US Army's ability to adapt to the vagaries of Counter-insurgency operations, *Learning to Eat Soup With a Knife*, "An Army codifies its institutional memory into doctrine."[11] Nagl goes on to quote from the 2001 edition of Field Manual 3-0, *Operations*, the Army's capstone directive on warfighting: "Army doctrine provides a common language and a common understanding of how Army forces conduct operations."[12]

Looking for the common language that Nagl refers to, it is possible to discern the genetic code of agility in the "flexible response" policy of the John F. Kennedy and Lyndon B. Johnson administrations of the early and mid-1960s. Faced with a bipolar strategic environment with the United States and the Soviet Union squared off in a permanent nuclear détente of deterrence and mutually assured destruction, defense policymakers strove to create additional scaled options for the President, options short of massive retaliation. The authors of the widely read security studies textbook, *American National Security*, wrote that "The strategy of flexible response was developed to give the President the capability to respond effectively to any challenge with the appropriate level of force" including the various responses of "massive retaliation, limited nuclear countervalue attacks, counterforce strikes, and. . . counter-insurgency."[13] In the face of an unknown and uncertain future, not only the possibility of a nuclear war with a peer adversary but also a potentially infinite array of challenges along the spectrum of force, defense planners developed a scaled menu of options, giving the President adaptable and nimble options to achieve victory or success. In this early appearance of an agility-like concept, two themes or patterns begin to emerge or coalesce: first, agility is as much an intellectual attribute as it is a physical one, having the capability to rapidly adapt and adjust to uncertainty and change, and second, agility is all about success, effectively adapting to change. In short, agility is about winning. Losers are not agile.

These two themes which underpin the concept of agility, agility as an intellectual capacity, and agility as inextricably linked to adapting to uncertainty and winning, manifest themselves in the sequential editions of the Army's capstone statement of its warfighting doctrine, *Field Manual 100-5, Operations*. In the edition of FM 100-5 published in 1976 with the memories of Vietnam still fresh in the institutional memory, the Army capstone operational document opens with a ringing clarion call that seeks to rebuke the stinging memory of Vietnam and its perception of defeat: "The Army's primary objective is to win the land battle—to fight and win in battles, large or small, against whatever foe, wherever we may be sent to war."[14] Indeed, as Nagl wrote, "the post-Vietnam Army intentionally turned away from the painful memories of its perceived losses in the collective Vietnam experience."[15] Indeed, in both the 1976 and 1982 revisions of FM 100-5, the senior leadership of the Army tried to achieve some measure of certainty by turning their back on the counter-insurgency of Vietnam, and attempting to isolate their mission by focusing their attention on defeating the Warsaw pact in Europe, while simultaneously ignoring or minimizing other potential global threats.[16] As the TRADOC official account of the evolution of doctrine acknowledges, this narrow focus caused much controversy not only within the Army, but also within the larger defense establishment.[17]

With the collapse of the Soviet Union and the end of the Cold War, the strategic environment grew more uncertain in mid 1990s, and agility manifested itself more insistently within US Army doctrine. Additionally, in the years since the mid-1980s, the US Army rather than limiting their prospective missions had undertaken more numerous and varied missions—Grenada (1983), Panama (1989), Kuwait (1990), and Somalia. With the collapse of the Soviet Union and the subsequent victory over Saddam Hussein's Republican Guard in Iraq in 1990, agility explodes into a position of doctrinal prominence in the mid-1990s with the next edition of FM 100-5. In strictly numerical terms, in the 1976 version where the army tried to limit uncertainty, the term agility (or agile) appears only 3 times; twenty years later, within the wide-open strategic environment, the use of agility (or agile) explodes, appearing ten times more frequently, a total of 35 appearances. Most importantly for our discussion, the concept of agility assumes a central position in the Army's thinking about how it fights in the mid-1990s, appearing as a foundational principle, one of 5 tenets of Army Operations: Initiative, Agility, Depth, Synchronization, and Versatility. Introducing the tenets of Army operations, the writers place them on the same plane as the time-tested and almost canonical Principles of War. Simultaneously acknowledging the greater range of missions that the Army could conceivably be called upon to execute, the manual states: "Victory is the objective, no matter the mission. . . . Nothing short of victory is acceptable."[18] The two intertwined themes of intellectual uncertainty and winning are evoked in the introduction. Closely linked to the principle of initiative, the manual defines agility as the:

> "Ability of friendly forces to react faster than the enemy and is a prerequisite for seizing and holding the initiative."

Additionally, the manual explicitly states that agility is as "much a mental as a physical quality."[19]

From the straightforward and simplistic dictionary definition of agility that we started with, we've seen that the Army doctrinal definition of agility over the years has added additional emphasis on the intellectual aspect of agility, implicitly alluding to the intellectual challenges of change and uncertainty, and additionally establishing a benchmark: agility is closely linked to success and winning. In the preface to his 2011 book, *The Agility Advantage: A Survival Guide for Complex Enterprises and Endeavors*, Alberts writes, "Agility is a difficult concept to appreciate because of its many facets . . . therefore, a quick look at the basic ideas associated with agility and its measurement may help some readers focus on the essence of agility."[20]

Starting from the common dictionary definition of agility, and having blended the additional themes apparent in the doctrinal definitions of agility as they have evolved over the last forty years—first, the intellectual and mental aspects of agility, and second, the implicit benchmark of effectiveness, success, and winning—we can now return to the original question about the definition of agility: can we adequately define agility within the context of the current strategic debate to achieve a common understanding of agility and its component attributes that meets the intent of our senior leaders?

Alberts proposes a common-sense definition of agility that effectively blends the dictionary and doctrinal definitions; he proposes the following definition:

"Agility is the ability to successfully effect, cope with, and/or exploit changes in circumstances."[21]

According to Alberts, agility is an umbrella concept that can be further broken down into subordinate component parts: responsiveness, versatility, flexibility, resilience, innovativeness, and adaptability.[22]

Starting from the dictionary definition of agility, and incorporating themes and elements from operational doctrine, this paper proposes a comprehensive working definition of agility:

> Agility is marked by a ready ability to physically move with quick easy grace; having a quick, resourceful, and adaptable intellectual character; nimbleness, dexterity; the ability to successfully effect, cope with, and/or exploit changes in circumstances; agility is comprised of component parts: responsiveness, versatility, flexibility, resilience, innovativeness, and adaptability.

Moving beyond the confines of the dictionary definition, and having arrived at a comprehensive working definition of agility that encompasses the essential attributes and components that our historical operational experience has codified into doctrine, are we any closer to providing a useful definition that will translate a concept into a practical roadmap? Although we have a more useful definition, this paper suggests that we should turn our attention to our most recent operational experiences in the counter-insurgency environments of Iraq and Afghanistan in order to contextualize agility within the hard earned lessons of our most recent combat experience; doing so should allow us to translate the abstract concept of agility into a concrete plan of action for future leaders.

Section 2. Agility in Action—Artfully Blending Lessons Learned to Achieve Pervasive Agility

"History not used is nothing, for all intellectual life is action, like practical life, and if you don't use the stuff well, it might as well be dead."[23]

--Arnold J. Toynbee, historian

"Well, what happened was, we got our ass kicked. In the second half, we just got our ass totally kicked. . . . The second half, we sucked. We couldn't stop the run. Every time they got the ball, they went down and got points. . . . It was a horseshit performance in the second half. Horseshit. I'm totally embarrassed and totally ashamed. Coaching did a horrible job. The players did a horrible job. . . . It sucked. It stunk."[24]

--Jim Mora, Head coach of the New Orleans Saints

Like a historian surveying the vast sweep of history and attempting to tease out patterns of causality across centuries, examining the rise, decline, and fall of civilizations, or a harried football coach assessing his defensive unit's dismal performance against the run, the Army is in a constant cycle of learning, conducting disciplined and detailed After Action Reviews (AARs) at the conclusion of every operation in an attempt to continue to learn, improve, and progress. Having established a working definition of agility that blends the positive attributes of the commonly understood dictionary definition of agility with the specialized connotations and themes that have evolved within our operational doctrine, we turn our attention to our recent operational experiences to assess agility within the context of our most recent combat experience. From this assessment, we should be able to discern exactly how our senior leaders want Army leaders to apply the concept of agility within the current strategic environment. Specifically, what lessons learned relating to agility can we draw from our recent operational experiences to guide leaders in their quest for agility in the future?

13

Objectively assessing the Army's performance over the last ten years, our nation's senior leaders have been overwhelming complimentary of our adaptability and flexibility as we have transformed from a Cold war army designed to execute combined arms maneuver in order to deter and defeat vast mobile formations on the plains of central Europe into a resilient Army that can detect and defeat complex insurgencies in the complex terrain of Iraq and Afghanistan. Indeed, as Secretary of Defense Leon Panetta stated in a speech to the senior leaders of the Association of the US Army in October 2011: "Over (the last) 10 years, we have become the best counterinsurgency force in the world, and we've also become the most adaptive, most expeditionary, and the most joint force in our country's history."[25]

In his previous role as the commanding general of Training and Doctrine Command (TRADOC), the current chairman of the Joint Chiefs of Staff, General Martin Dempsey presided over the publication of a series of forward-looking doctrinal manuals, the TRADOC 525-3 series which includes the *US Army Capstone Concept*, and the *US Army Operating Concept;* the series also includes nested documents that propose how the subordinate war fighting functions will doctrinally support the overall conceptual framework. Commenting on the Army's successful adaptations to the counterinsurgency environments in Iraq and Afghanistan, the *Army Capstone concept* noted that: "Essential elements of successful operations in Iraq included a keen understanding of the situation, integration of all arms and joint capabilities, the development and integration of indigenous forces, and military support to governance and development. Most important was the ability to adapt operations continuously as forces developed the situation through action."[26]

As General Robert Cone, the current TRADOC Commander stated, "Once the insurgency broke out, we struggled to find an appropriate doctrinal approach to guide us to a solution."[27] In the initial stages of Operation Iraqi Freedom, the Army and its warfighting organizations (Divisions and Brigades), designed as they were for combined arms maneuver, organized, equipped and trained to defeat mobile armored formations in open terrain, struggled to come to grips with an enemy and environment that they weren't prepared for.

Holistically, the Army as a total force has been praised for its adaptability. Using our working definition of agility to assess operations, let's drill down on a specific subset of Soldiers, leaders, and units in order to avoid generalizations and draw out specific examples of agility to objectively determine the nature of and quality of agility displayed. This paper will focus on units and organizations of the field artillery, units typically charged with carrying out the specialized tasks categorized under the fires warfighting function, one of six doctrinal warfighting functions along with mission command, movement and maneuver, intelligence, sustainment, and protection. Army Doctrinal Publication 3-0, *Unified Land Operations*, defines the fires warfighting function as the related tasks and systems that provide collective and coordinated use of Army indirect fires, air and missile defense, and joint fires through the targeting process.[28] As previously stated, this paper will focus on the fires warfighting function for two reasons: first, to allow a more specific analysis of agility by focusing on Soldiers, leaders, and units tasked to perform a specific function within the umbrella concept of unified land operations; second, because the counter-insurgency campaigns of the last decade arguably placed greater demands on the agility of the fires warfighting function and artillerymen than other branches or functions. In counterinsurgency operations, massed field artillery fires, while highly destructive and effective in a conventional sense, are actually counterproductive to achieving tactical, operational, and strategic objectives. Consequently, in counterinsurgency operations of both Iraq and Afghanistan, field artilleryman and fire supporters were under tremendous pressure to adapt to contribute to the overall mission. Because of this, fires organizations and fire support leaders and Soldiers at all echelons were on the cutting edge of the transformations that led ultimately to the Army's success. Although every Soldier, every leader, every unit of every type, military branch, and specialty had to adapt on some level to achieve success in a counterinsurgency environment, field artillerymen and fires organizations are perhaps the best candidate for a collective case study of the nature and quality of applied agility.

Drawing on the intellectual component of agility, the recognition of changed conditions, and the subsequent need to adapt in order to win, fires organizations and fire supporters were among the first units and Soldiers to demonstrate an effective adaptation to the combat environment. As Brigade Combat Team commanders found themselves responsible for vast stretches of complex terrain, and they identified that they lacked sufficient combat power to effectively engage the elusive enemy hiding among the population, they recognized that massed artillery fires were not an integral part of daily operations. Consequently, brigade combat team commanders task organized fires battalions as maneuver battle space owners, giving fires battalions full responsibility for all lines of effort (security, partnership, legitimate governance, and economic development) within that battlespace. A change in mission of this magnitude required a wholesale transformation and adaptation down to the DNA level of the fires organizations—from fires battalion battle staffs executing decentralized mission command to howitzer sections and cannon crewmembers or fire direction specialists reorganizing as infantry squads and performing room clearing operations as a member of a reorganized infantry squad. Using our working definition to assess their adjustments, artillerymen and fires leaders effectively coped with uncertainty and changing circumstances by nimbly adapting to the demands of the environment, parking their howitzers and cannons, and dexterously assuming other combat roles.

Across ten years and countless formations in both the active and reserve forces, this adaptability migrated to follow-on units. As the conflicts in both theaters continued and widened, the adaptability of fires units continued through subsequent deployments. From the earliest days of Operation Iraqi Freedom (OIF) and Enduring Freedom (OEF), Fires Brigades and Battalions of all types have performed similar missions in both theaters throughout both campaigns. Confident in the ability and agility of fires brigades and battalions, these units routinely served as maneuver forces all through the end of OIF and continuing today in OEF. Fires brigades and battalions have performed other adaptations to meet the demands of other missions as the combat environment dictated: as base defense operations cells (BDOCs), or as transportation units, or as target acquisition batteries, or as military police or detention facility guards.

Simultaneously, fire supporters on staffs at all echelons who were not engaged in their anticipated core competency of planning, synchronizing, and executing lethal fires in support of maneuver forces, adjusted their operations to emphasize the targeting process. At the brigade and battalion level, fire supporters lead the effort to adapt the

17

Decide-Detect-Deliver-Assess process (D3A) to focus the brigade's effort not only on lethal effects, but they also expanded the process to include full spectrum effects (personality targeting, information operations, civil military operations, public affairs, money as a weapon system). At the company level, fire supporters lead the effort to develop bottom-up driven intelligence capabilities, and in many BCTs, Company Intelligence Support Teams (COISTs) are routinely manned by the Company Fire Support Team (Company FIST).

Looking closely at our definition of agility, artillerymen in both theaters displayed intellectual and physical acuity, identified the components of the changing environment, and nimbly and effectively adjusted their operations accordingly to achieve success; field artillerymen were responsive, versatile, flexible, resilient, innovative, and adaptable. To cite the accomplishments of just one field artillery battalion among hundreds as an example of agility, the 4th Battalion, 42d Field Artillery (4-42 FA), the Straight Arrows, were at least partially responsible for the capture of Saddam Hussein in December of 2003. Assigned to the 1st Brigade Combat Team of the 4th Infantry Division, the Soldiers and leaders of 4-42 FA had nimbly adapted their operations to the exigencies of the tactical situation, reorganized from an M109A6 Paladin battalion into a multi-functional maneuver battalion, and effectively operated as the battlespace owner in eastern Salah-ah-Din province which encompassed the former dictator's home town of Ad Dawr, his ultimate place of capture.[29] Without identifying the artillerymen of the "Straight Arrow" battalion, the authors of *On Point II*, a history of Operation Iraqi Freedom published by the Combat Studies Institute at Fort Leavenworth, called attention to the intellectual agility of the unit, writing: "Saddam's detention resulted from months of careful intelligence work by the CJTF-7 staff, US Special Operations Forces, and especially the Soldiers of 4ID who were operating in the Sunni heartland."[30]

Acknowledging the changed mission set of field artillery Soldiers, leaders, and units, General Raymond Odierno, currently serving as the Army Chief of Staff, commented on the performance of artillery organizations under his command in the 4th Infantry Division in the Sunni Triangle region in North Central Iraq during the first year of the war (2003-04). In an interview in *Field Artillery Journal*, he said: "Artillery has to be a versatile asset. The Army can no longer afford to have artillerymen just do artillery missions." Addressing the specific requirements that the counterinsurgency environment placed on artillery units, he continued: "Every one of my artillery battalions owned battlespace. My FA battalions were just like my maneuver battalions. That's the kind of flexibility we need as we look to the future."[31] Interestingly, General Odierno used language that appears in our working definition of agility—versatility, and flexibility—in his description of artillery operations, Soldiers, and leaders.

While not an all-encompassing accounting of fires adaptability over the last ten years, these examples clearly demonstrate that soldiers and leaders within the fires warfighting function, and field artilleryman in particular have proven to be adaptable. But does the example of field artilleryman and fires in Iraq and Afghanistan serve as the singular example of agility *par excellence* as we look for the future?

The short answer is no. Without minimizing the accomplishments of artillerymen over the last decade, their adaptations were limited in nature to the specific requirements of the counter-insurgency environment and don't provide a good model for the agility that will be needed for the future. More importantly, the adjustments made by artilleryman in Iraq and Afghanistan over the last ten years are substantively different from the essence of agility that our senior leaders envision (in accordance with our working definition of agility). Indeed, in a series of articles in *Army* magazine that were written to clarify and reinforce the message of agility and adaptability of the Capstone Concept series of pamphlets to a wider audience of Army leaders, General Dempsey went on to say that these ideas—operational adaptability, agility and versatility—are "not yet institutionalized in our doctrine and our training—they do not yet 'pervade the force.'"[32]

The agility that we demonstrated so ably in the counter-insurgency (COIN) environment was a limited agility, a series of one-way and semi-permanent transformations and adaptations. The US Army's COIN doctrine required a "limited agility." Looking at our working definition of agility, the previously discussed adaptations were based not on uncertainty, but on the certainty that fires would not be needed— more specifically, adaptations were based on the certainty that fires would not be needed in the volumes required to adequately support combined arms maneuver. As the previous discussion of adaptations within the fires community have demonstrated, these adaptations and transformations were done to implement an evolving COIN strategy and in response to local conditions of mission, enemy, terrain, troops and time available, and civil considerations (METT-TC). When Brigades assigned fires battalions maneuver missions and firing batteries transformed into maneuver companies, leaders were certain that they would not need to mass field artillery battalions in support of combined arms maneuver, and they assumed that these transformations would last throughout the duration of the deployment. Indeed, as fires organizations transformed and adapted to the COIN environment, they largely surrendered the competencies required of their previous fires function.

In short, these combat adaptations, these demonstrations of agility, were one-way and semi-permanent. To be clear, that is less than the "pervasive agility" that our senior leaders envision, and that the future will require. The uncertainty of the future will require the Army as a whole, and its fires forces in particular to be even more agile, the agility of our working definition.

With our definition of agility in mind, it is appropriate to ask what sort of uncertain environment and operational environment and mission set our senior leader propose for us to be ready for. Preliminary answers can be found not only in the aforementioned *Priorities for 21st Century Defense,* but also in *Unified Land Operations (Army Doctrine Publication 3-0),* and *The Army Operating Concept (TRADOC PAM 525-3-1)*, the doctrinal roadmap that describes how the Army will fight. Both *Unified Land Operations* and The *Operating Concept* describe an operational environment that will require an Army that is agile and adaptable enough to execute decisive action by means of complementary core competencies: combined arms maneuver (CAM), the application . . . of combat power to achieve advantage over the enemy, and wide area security (WAS), the application . . . of combat power in coordination with other military and civilian capabilities to deny the enemy positions of advantage, protect forces, populations, infrastructure and activities and consolidate tactical and operational gains to set conditions for achieving strategic and policy goals.[33]

Explaining the logic behind the evolving doctrine, General Robert Cone, the commander of the Army Training and Doctrine Command, wrote that the dual core competencies of decisive action, combined arms maneuver and wide area security, "capture the lessons learned from our recent past and artfully blends them with the broader precepts of warfighting." [34] In other words, the Army must be able to anticipate and adapt to changing battlefield conditions; the Army must be nimble, dexterous, able to transition rapidly between CAM and WAS, between one extreme and the other—or even more likely, be prepared to execute both simultaneously.

The pervasive agility that our senior leaders are looking for takes the best practices demonstrated by the Army holistically and Soldiers, leaders and units of the Field Artillery and the Fires Warfighting function in particular over the last ten years of Counterinsurgency, and combines them with the elements of agility of our working definition. Our definition of agility, in line with General Dempsey's pervasive agility fully encompasses the limited adaptability and agility that drove our adaptations in support of operations in Iraq and Afghanistan, and is fundamentally different, more expansive, and more inclusive. General Dempsey stated in his foreword to the *Capstone Concept*, that operational adaptability and agility will "require a mindset based on flexibility of thought calling for leaders at all levels who are comfortable with collaborative planning and decentralized execution, have a tolerance for ambiguity, and possess the ability and willingness to make rapid adjustments according to the situation."[35] The Chairman's vision for a pervasive agility is, to be candid, a more agile agility. General Raymond Odierno, the current Army Chief of Staff elaborated in his marching orders, "we must be flexible in the face of adversity and agile in our responsiveness, able to dominate any operational environment against conventional and hybrid threats."

In short, agility for the future enables and empowers the Army's ability to seamlessly transition between combined arms maneuver and wide area security. In the past, we've searched for certainty as we prepared our forces for combat. We've made assumptions about the nature of the enemy and gambled on the nature of the conflict. We won't have that luxury in the future. According to General Cone, "prior to 2003, we focused almost entirely on major combat operations; since then, primarily on counter-insurgency."[36] As General Dempsey said in a speech in November 2011, "We're never going to try to build a force that's only capable of doing one thing at a time. That would be silly."[37]

Having arrived at a working definition of agility and then closely analyzed our operations over the last ten years of counter-insurgency in accordance with that definition, it's possible to discern that there is a rift between the agility that we've celebrated in Iraq and Afghanistan and the pervasive agility that our senior leaders are describing for future operations. So how do we close that gap? In the final section, we'll leverage the close analysis of the fires warfighting function from this section with proposed priorities for developing a practical roadmap to achieving pervasive agility.

Section 3. Agility in Practice—Drafting a Roadmap to Pervasive Agility

"When a man finds himself in motion, he always thinks up a goal for that motion. One needs a vision of the promised land in order to have the strength to move."[38]
--Leo Tolstoy

"Two roads diverged in a wood, and I—I took the one less traveled by, and that has made all the difference."[39]
--Robert Frost

Future generations of Americans will hold us accountable for the decisions and actions of today. As our nation's leaders have directed, in this new age of uncertainty and interconnectedness, agility is not a luxury; it's a necessity. As Alberts wrote, "Our ability to predict, and hence to plan, has been greatly diminished as a consequence of the complexity and dynamics of our environments and the nature of the responses necessary to survive and prosper. Survival in this new age requires, above all else, agility."[40]

With the stakes of failure so high, the problem of uncertainty is especially acute for our Armed Forces. As a nation, our track record of adequately preparing our armed forces for the next armed conflict is not good. As General Dempsey stated in a speech in 2009:"Generally speaking, we normally get the future wrong. We don't get it wrong intentionally, and we don't get it wrong dramatically in most cases. But we do get it wrong."[41] In an age of uncertainty, the only certainty is that we will guess incorrectly as we try to ascertain the nature of future threats. Agility as we've defined it is a way to hedge our bets.

Having developed a comprehensive working definition of agility and placed it within the context of our recent operational experience and within the current strategic debate, let's move on to the future of agility: So more specifically, what does agility mean in practical terms to future Army leaders? How do we artfully blend lessons

24

learned from the last ten years with our traditional core warfighting competencies to achieve agility? Using our working definition, can we draft a practical roadmap to achieve agility?

> Agility is marked by a ready ability to physically move with quick easy grace; having a quick, resourceful, and adaptable intellectual character; nimbleness, dexterity; the ability to successfully effect, cope with, and/or exploit changes in circumstances; agility is comprised of component parts: responsiveness, versatility, flexibility, resilience, innovativeness, and adaptability.

Two things to capture here before we move on: first, our working definition of agility appears to be the appropriate solution to address a doctrinal need, the ability to anticipate and seamlessly transition between the extremes of the Army's potential employment in unified land operations and decisive action. Our Army must be agile enough to execute combined arms maneuver and wide area security. Being able to execute both ends of spectrum competently is a given; that is not agility. Being agile is the ability to do one, or the other, or both simultaneously, and being able to anticipate and move between the two seamlessly. Second, as we look to the future, agility poses intellectual and physical challenges to all Army organizations at all echelons and in each of the warfighting functions; Agility applies to all Soldiers, leaders of every military occupational specialty, branch, and functional area, and units of every type. However, the following discussion of the demands, challenges, and priorities of addressing agility within the fires warfighting function and field artillery units may provide a useful starting point for units of all types across the Army. Agility may pose an especially daunting challenge to fires organizations: to fires organizations, the two ends of the spectrum present a potentially paralyzing array of combat tasks—from providing massed artillery fires in support of combined arms maneuver—circa 2000—to the battle-space owning

25

maneuver task force of the fires battalion in wide area security—circa 2003 to the present in the COIN campaigns of Iraq and Afghanistan. To a combined arms battalion commander, the transition between combined arms maneuver and wide area security is conceptual; subordinate elements will execute combat tasks that are within the same range of maneuver tasks, the same family of skills. On the other hand, a fires leader who visualizes this same transition perceives a much wider variety of tasks: the need to mass fires at the decisive point in support of combined arms maneuver, and the small unit patrolling and maneuver tasks of COIN, implied for wide area security. Telling a fires Soldier that he must be agile is telling him to drink the ocean through a straw. Discussing agility in the context of fires will be useful for all Soldiers and leaders.

Revisiting our working definition and keeping in mind the strategic imperative of the dual core competencies of decisive action, three broad priorities for fires leaders, Soldiers, and organizations emerge: 1) enable agility by focusing on the fundamentals of the fires warfighting function across the spectrum; 2) build agile organizations—alert to changing circumstances: adaptable, nimble, versatile, and flexible; and 3) practice agility by establishing and enforcing versatile standards and processes.

Priority 1—Enable Agility by Focusing on the Fundamentals of the Fires Warfighting Function. Pervasive agility in the fires warfighting function will require an agile fires mindset, leaders who have visualized the fight at both ends of the spectrum and who own the warfighting function across the extremes of combined arms maneuver and wide area security, who have re-mastered both the technical science of indirect fires gunnery and the art of tactical fires integration. This underlying competence will be the foundation upon which agility can be built.

BG Thomas Vandal, the former commandant of the Field Artillery School, wrote, "We must recapture the core competencies that combined arms maneuver will require without surrendering the flexibility and versatility to provide responsive fires in a wide area security environment. In short, we must recapture our ability to "shoot, move, and communicate." Vandal goes on to say: "we must dedicate ourselves to recapture our ability to apply the five requirements of accurate predictive fire, to integrate fires with maneuver, and to improve our ability to shoot and move . . . this must be our *first priority* to reestablish our preeminence as the *King of Battle* for our maneuver brothers."[42]

Focus on the Fundamentals of the Warfighting function. First and foremost, fires leaders must own the fires warfighting function again. Fires leaders must embrace the definition of agility and visualize what both core competencies will require from fires, from the centralized massed fires of combined arms maneuver to the dispersed and decentralized fires of wide area security. Pervasive agility will require fires organizations that can provide fires in both extremes simultaneously or can nimbly transition between the two. Within the context of the brigade combat team, fires battalion commanders need to redefine the role of the Fire Support Coordinator (FSCOORD), and work with the Brigade Commander and staff to provide training oversight and supervision of the subordinate elements that are responsible for executing the fires function.

Over the last decade of deployments into the counter-insurgency environment of Iraq and Afghanistan, the fires function has been competing for the attention of fires leaders with the other demands of COIN: maneuver missions, base defense operations, full spectrum targeting, civil military operations, bottom-up driven intelligence collection and analysis, etc. A parallel transformation that occurred during this timeframe that had second order effects on the fires warfighting function was the transformation to the modular Brigade Combat Team (BCT); under the modular BCT, the Army organized fire supporters under their maneuver headquarters, removing the fires battalion commander and the fires battalion from the direct chain of responsibility for the fires function. Looking at the extremes of combined arms maneuver and wide area security, it is possible to infer that combined arms maneuver will require more centralized mission command to achieve the BCT commander's intent. Fires in support of combined arms maneuver will also require more centralized control. As we take the lessons learned from wide area security and move back to Combined Arms Maneuver, we will need to reassert our ownership of the fires function, recognizing that the fires warfighting function cuts across all of the formations in the BCT. Indeed, all of the warfighting functions cut across all of the formations within the BCT and may require adjustments of duties and responsibilities within other organizations across the BCT, the brigade support battalion commander and the subordinate forward support company commanders within the context of the sustainment warfighting function, for example. This will be a change within the BCT; to offset the shock of this change, a fires battalion commander taking an active role in managing and training the fire supporters within the BCT, fires battalion commanders need to demonstrate value-added to the combined arms battalions and the cavalry squadron through training oversight of the fire supporters within the Brigade combat team. Once maneuver commanders experience more effective fires during combined arms maneuver operations through more effectively trained fire supporters and more effective centralized control of massed fires, greater, they'll prove to be more receptive to a more centralized mission command of the fires function.

Reclaim the science of the Gunnery Solution. With a high percentage of field artilleryman and fire supporters of all grades and military occupational specialties performing non-standard missions over the last decade, we have a generation of field artillerymen who have missed a decade of development and experience in the practical science of the delivery of indirect fires. We have field grade officers whose experience of command was commanding an artillery battery transformed into a motorized-infantry company; in effect, they've never commanded a firing battery, have never massed fires, have never faced the intellectual challenge of troubleshooting the elements of the five requirements of accurate predicted fire to achieve target effects. Likewise, we will have firing platoon sergeants who have never served as howitzer section chiefs, who have never supervised a howitzer section in the execution of the basics of TLABSPAP (Trails, Lay, Aiming points, Boresight, Safe, Prefire checks, Ammunition preparation, and Position improvement).

Pervasive agility will require not only that we recapture the competencies of massing fires, but also that we capture and inculcate the gunnery lessons from the last decade of wide area security; some key takeaways are our improvements in timely and precise reactive counter-fire, distributed fires in support of dispersed operating bases, and the practical techniques of precision fires. As an example of artful blending of lessons learned from the wide area security environment, as we move back to combined arms maneuver, we will need to sustain and promulgate across the breadth of our formations the tactics and procedures of employing precision munitions

(Excalibur and GMLRS). Within the budget constraints that our Army will face, this pollenization may require creative measures, perhaps virtual or constructive scenarios. The National Training Center at Fort Irwin, California, with its vast terrain and immersive training environment, can assist by providing an opportunity for live fire that not only trains the firing unit (at least one howitzer section), but also the entire brigade combat team from mission command and sensor to shooter linkages in a live scenario.

Recover the art of Fires support integration/synchronization into combined arms maneuver. Combined arms maneuver will present fires organizations with operations that have a more complex scheme of maneuver, a more rapid operational tempo, and with greater possibilities for sequels and exploitation. Pervasive agility will require fire supporters to more actively integrate fires into the scheme of maneuver during planning and preparation for operations. Over the last ten years, there has been an attrition of fires planning skills. The ability to develop fire support tasks from the top, and refine them through bottom-up planning and rehearsals has atrophied. Pervasive agility will require fire supporters who retain the wide area security skills that they have developed—the full spectrum targeting process, specific functional expertise (information operations, civil-military operations, public affairs operations, intelligence analysis etc.), but also rediscover the fundamentals of fires integration. There are multiple skills that need to be recaptured in the fire support realm, but let's focus on one: rehearsals. From observations of units at the NTC, a decade of wide area security operations has desensitized leaders within the BCT to the efficacy of the fire support rehearsal. As we move forward, fires leaders would do well to focus energy on reviving and reintegrating fire support rehearsals into BCT mission preparation timelines, not merely a cursory discussion of fires at the combined arms rehearsal (CAR), but rather a detailed rehearsal of fires either within the CAR or a separate fires rehearsal with maneuver leaders. A useful mnemonic to revive: PLOT-CR (Purpose of fires, Location of fires, Observer, Triggers, Communications, Resources available—or the competing mnemonic TTLODAC if you prefer). More complex fires in support of higher tempo maneuver operations will require not only better synchronization across the warfighting functions, but also a more complete dissemination and situational understanding of fires among all leaders; reclaim our reputation of 24/7 reliability by continuing this rehearsal of fires from a map board/terrain model rehearsal to a technical rehearsal that not only validates the gunnery solution for individual targets, exercises communications linkages between sensor and shooter, and also clarifies tactical and technical triggers for specific targets.

One further problem that agility presents to a fires soldier is a perception of the relevance of fires in wide area security. In the COIN environment of Iraq, an attendant myth grew that wide area security equals less fires. Moving forward, we need to explore and expose this myth; fires in support of wide area security operations are different from fires in support of combined arms maneuver, but just as central to the successful prosecution of operations: more discriminate, more precise, more exactly timed.

Artful blending of lessons learned will require bringing forward lessons learned that may be difficult to sustain. As examples, here are two that we must strive to sustain: the integration of joint fires and the sensitivity to collateral damage. First, we know that the Army as a part of unified land operations will not fight alone in the future; it will be a joint environment, and we must retain the skills that we have refined over the last ten years in leveraging the capabilities of joint platforms. The training and qualification of Joint Forward Observers (JFOs) is costly and intensive; it's worth the investment, though. Second, any adversary that we may face in the future will leverage complex urban terrain and intermingled civilian populations to limit our ability to maneuver and apply fires. We need to sustain the sensitivity and techniques of collateral damage estimates to minimize the negative consequences of unintended collateral damage. Through ten years of operations in a restrictive fires environment with the attendant hypersensitivity to collateral damage, we've become proficient in collateral damage analysis in our fire support elements; simultaneously, we've developed operating procedures for disseminating the potential risk of collateral damage to maneuver commanders who can make informed decisions about the risk and reward of attacking targets with various methods of fires. This is hard work; but as we've learned, an agile enemy will use any mistakes that we make in this arena to create exponentially devastating effects against us in the information domain. It would be a shame to walk away from this hard earned competency thinking that we won't need it again.

Agility is about winning. Agility will require leaders who visualize both ends of the spectrum, and build the competencies to operate effectively in both environments—combined arms maneuver and wide area security. This wide ranging technical and tactical competence—whether in the fires warfighting function, as discussed above, or in the mission command, maneuver, intelligence, sustainment, or protection warfighting functions—will require engaged leaders who artfully blend the hard fought lessons learned of the last ten years counterinsurgency with the traditional core competencies of high intensity conflict.

Priority 2— Build agile fires organizations—alert to changing circumstances: adaptable, nimble, versatile, and flexible. Pervasive agility will demand nimble, responsive, versatile and flexible fires organizations that can not only execute fires in support of both core competencies, but also the more variegated skills that we have accrued over ten years of wide area security operations. Fires leaders should seek to revisit the lessons learned of combined arms maneuver while retaining the non-traditional skills of wide area security operations, and then strive to create versatile and flexible units that can execute both. Agile fires organizations must prepare to execute core competencies at both ends of the spectrum, and nimbly transition between centralized and decentralized operations, grounded in the broad base of tactical fundamentals, and avoiding the trap of specialization. Anticipation and responsiveness will be key components of our ability to successfully execute these transitions.

Build agile formations prepared to execute core competencies and prioritized non-traditional tasks. As leaders visualize the extremes of both core competencies to build agile formations, we should establish priorities in order to avoid overloading ourselves with "essential tasks," and risk paralyzing ourselves. Focus on the fundamentals; look for the commonalities across the spectrum of conflict, both delivering and integrating fires in support of the extremes of combined arms maneuver to wide area security. According to the *Army Operating Concept,* both combined arms maneuver and wide area security will possess elements of offensive operations, defensive operation, and stability and support operations. Furthermore, the Operating

Concept explains that both combined arms maneuver and wide area security both possess "similar core elements such as combined arms competency, effective reconnaissance and security operations, and the need to seize and retain the initiative."[43] Fires are instrumental in the successful prosecution of all of these operations. Fires organizations, not only units focused on delivery of field artillery fires such as fires battalion and firing batteries, platoons and howitzer sections of all types but also fire support elements from the brigade to the Task Force and down to the platoon and forward observer team, should strive to rebuild their core competencies of shoot, move, and communicate. However, we can't simply turn back the clock to recapture our core competencies. Recognizing that full spectrum operations will require the agility to move between the two extremes, leaders within the brigade combat team will need to prioritize the non-traditional skills that we've accrued over the last ten years of wide area security operations. For firing units, COIN patrolling and host nation security force partnership may occupy the top of the list; for fire supporters at all echelons, the full spectrum targeting process, focused functional specialties such as information operations, civil-military affairs, and public affairs, and bottom-up intelligence collection and analysis should head the list.

Build agile modular formations to facilitate decentralized operations and rapid transitions. In full spectrum operations, we must be prepared to nimbly execute rapid transitions between combined arms maneuver and wide area security. Pervasive agility will demand that we have flexible and standardized modular formations that are prepared to rapidly adjust their task organization in order to support more centralized combined arms maneuver and more decentralized wide area security, and every possible permutation in between the two extremes. The underpinning principle of standardization underpins modularity: in theory, standardized and self-sufficient modular brigade combat teams can plug and play into any Joint task organization. The same principle would lead me to recommend that fires leaders build and develop agile modular formations that facilitate the rapid adaptability of frequent task organization changes. As an example of extremely agile and flexible task organization: Firing battalions should be prepared to mass fires in support of combined arms maneuver from multiple firing units, as well as providing dispersed firing elements of potentially different sized formations—two to four gun platoons—in support of ongoing wide area security operations. Depending on the mission, the enemy, the terrain and weather, time, troops available and civil considerations (METT-TC), pervasive agility should drive field artillery battalions to develop the flexibility to consolidate into firing batteries to mass fires, or conversely starburst out into two to four gun platoons to support specific combined arms maneuver or wide area security operations. In order to facilitate this decentralized task organization, develop a standard template for self-sufficient two gun platoons with fire direction capability and sustainment operations. At the lower end of the wide area security mission, pervasive agility and the lessons learned from the previous ten years would lead the battalion to retain the capability to selectively transform firing platoons (or elements from firing platoons, or individual Soldiers from firing platoons) into maneuver platoons in order to sustain a maneuver capability to perform tasks as a maneuver task force—partnership, security, key leader engagements, civil military operations, information operations, etc. . . . At the very least, the battalion will potentially need the ability to conduct local force protection and sustainment functions such as a forward operating base quick reaction force or combat logistics patrol. The more versatile and more flexible an organization can be, the better. No one ever said that agility would be easy; establishing priorities will be key.

Avoid creating specialized units that limit flexibility. Lastly, we should strive to avoid the trap of creating functionally specialized units that limit the flexibility and operational adaptability of fires organizations. For a firing battalion, there will be a tendency to create firing pure batteries and platoons and maneuver pure batteries (companies) and platoons, enabling leaders and Soldiers to focus on a limited set of tasks and to train to achieve a deeper and more comprehensive expertise on that more limited set of tasks. Unfortunately, this specialization limits the overall flexibility and agility of the fires warfighting function. Pervasive agility will drive us to retain flexibility by retaining multifunctional units—batteries and platoons that can serve as firing elements, and/or as maneuver elements and headquarters. For fire supporters, we need to remember that we best contribute to our supported maneuver unit's success in decisive action by giving them fully functional fires. We need to be grounded in the fundamentals of fire support. We must contribute by providing the non-standard tasks that we have accrued over the last ten years; however, we need to develop a backup plan, a bench that is prepared to perform those tasks so that we can ensure the fires function is serviced first and always. As an example, many brigade combat teams routinely employ their company fire support teams (FIST) as the Company Intelligence Support Team (COISTs) in a wide area security operational environment. Company FISTs have performed magnificently in this role in both theaters, and Fire Support Soldiers are the absolutely logical choice to employ in this critical combat role. Pervasive agility, however, should drive unit leaders to develop a transition plan for their fire supporters to hand off this responsibility in the event of a combined arms maneuver operation that requires observed and synchronized fires. The same battle handover plan applies to fire supporters at all echelons; pervasive agility must prevent us from assuming non-standard roles and combat tasks that we cannot hand off.

Priority 3— Practice agility by establishing and enforcing versatile standards and processes. My final recommendation to fires leaders as they prioritize their efforts to create pervasive agility is the establishment and enforcement of standards and standard operating procedures (SOPs) that support pervasive agility and adaptability. We establish the foundations of our combat readiness in training; we must train as we plan to fight, and we must create standards that will enhance our agility, that is our ability to operate effectively in both core competencies and at any point and permutation in between. The final recommendation here is twofold: first, I recommend that leaders focus on developing standards that support operations at both end of the spectrum and the transition between the extremes, and second, establish standards that enhance agile mission command—the transition from centralized to decentralized mission command.

Agile Standard Operating Procedures. Pervasive agility will demand units that are prepared to execute both core competencies; fires leaders should strive to establish standard operating procedures that are agile enough to support both ends, and the transition between the two extremes. At the NTC, the key difference that separated units that struggled from units that were well prepared to execute their combat tasks was the establishment, dissemination, and deep understanding of standards within the organization. I had the privilege to serve at the NTC at the tail end of our involvement in Iraq and during the surge into Afghanistan, and the Army Force Generation Process produced units that arrived at the NTC for their mission readiness exercise at varying degrees of readiness. Due to anomalies in the ARFORGEN process, some units arrived more seasoned and mature than others, with multiple combat rotations, stable leaders in key positions, and on a fairly predictable deployment and dwell time ratio. Other units arrived at the NTC newly-formed with sparse organizational continuity. While all units departed prepared to execute their combat mission, the units that benefitted the most from the intensive collective experience at the NTC were the units that arrived with the more complete set of understood standard operating procedures. They were able to use the training event to refine their SOPs and more deeply ingrain those standards into the DNA of their unit. Units that were developing their SOPs and learning them while at the NTC, departed for combat with fewer repetitions of "what right looks like," and a shallower dissemination of the standard across their formation. Knowing the broad outline of their prospective mission, leaders did a magnificent job training their organizations on the tasks, and the task organization of their understood mission. Artfully blending the lessons learned from the past ten years should lead us to establish standards and standard operating procedures that will prepare us for any environment, any threat, any mission. SOPs need to address the agility required to operate at both ends of the spectrum and the transitions between the two. Most firing units that I observed at the NTC possessed SOPs that were either largely maneuver-centric Standard Operating Procedures (SOPs,) developed from previous combat rotations, or purely fires-centric SOPS, vestiges from pre-OIF/OEF days, culled from the depths of a

38

database buried in the Battalion S-3 shop. Pervasive agility will require the artful blending of these two documents.

My recommendation to fires leaders would be to establish standards that support operations at both ends of the spectrum. Focus on the platoon as the centerpiece of battalion operations and establish rock-solid standards for task organization and operations. Common standards will reduce friction and allow dynamic task organization changes, allowing platoons to operate under the battalion or battery direction for massed fires under the centralized control of combined arms maneuver, and also reduce friction as we starburst out platoons to support individual task forces or smaller units in support of wide area security. Focus on platoon standards that support both core competencies. As an example, establish clearly understood standards for every step in the troop leading procedures—Operations orders, rehearsals, pre-combat checks, and then ruthlessly enforce them to ensure deep understanding down to the Soldier level. Troop leading procedures should be the foundation of our operations, whether as a firing platoon supporting combined arms maneuver, or as a platoon operating in a firing/maneuver capacity as a part of decentralized task organized dispersed wide area security environment.

Agile Mission Command. The mission command warfighting function, since it underpins all other warfighting functions, is probably most impacted by the requirements of pervasive agility. As we artfully blend the lessons learned from the last ten years, we must pay attention to the requirements of mission command as we develop an ability to seamlessly transition between the two extremes and the combinations in between. Combined arms maneuver requires a more centralized and mobile mission command.

Over the last ten years of wide area security operations, we have refined and established mature mission command systems over dispersed operating bases that provide real time situational awareness over a blended array of automated systems—command post of the future (CPOF), blue forces tracker (BLUFOR tracker), elements of the Army Battle Command System (ABCS) to include the Advanced Field Artillery Tactical Data System (AFATDS), with other non-standard systems to include chat functions (Jabberchat, MircChat, and others), intelligence systems (TIGR net and CIDNE, and mapping tools (Falconview and C2PC). The challenge as we move back to centralized command and control and more mobile operations will be bandwidth as we prioritize what tools to push forward into mobile command posts in support of combined arms maneuver. The "communicate" of shoot, move, and communicate is much more technically challenging now as we move back to tactical radio operations, whether it will be on the ASIP radio, the Joint Integrated Tactical Radio (JITR), or some other platform. Based on observations from the NTC, units will have a hard time reestablishing mastery of FM communications, especially as part of a distributed network that will encompass combined arms maneuver and ongoing wide area security counterfire radar networks. This is a technical problem, and leaders will need to dig in and get their hands dirty as we grapple with the problems of communicating complex data sets in real time across dispersed forces in support of decentralized operations.

But this is not merely a technical problem; it's also tactical and procedural, and as we address mission command for combined arms operations, we cannot neglect the lessons learned over the last ten years in managing airspace. We are exponentially more sensitive to the challenges of integrating indirect fires into a complex airspace

40

environment populated by joint and army fixed and rotary platforms, as well as multiple unmanned aircraft, not to mention civilian air traffic. We cannot assume away complicated airspace and regress to simplistic solutions of previous eras. Similarly, with the non-linear battlefield of the wide area security environment, fire supporters will need to dust off fire support coordination measures and reintegrate their use into combined arms maneuver; we have a generation of fire supporters who do not understand the utility of a coordinated fire line. Artfully blending the ingenious solutions that fire supporters have devised over the last decade to clear ground and airspace in a non-linear environment is the absolute distillation of pervasive agility.

Fires leaders should establish standard mission command procedures that facilitate both core competencies. Flexible battle rhythm with nested reporting is one example. With the decentralized operations of wide area security, BCTs and fires battalions were not engaged with maintaining situational understanding of the fires warfighting function, and they consequently did not maintain an accurate common operational picture (COP) or running estimate of fires assets—ammunition availability, metro dissemination, class V distribution, ammunition lots, precision munition availability, fires assets maintenance issues—howitzers, mortars, observation platforms (Melios, BFIST) . Establishing standard reports specifically addressing fires assets and readiness from subordinate units nested into the BCT battle rhythm will address this problem. Accurate running estimates will be absolutely required to facilitate the rapid transitions from wide area security to combined arms maneuver and the dynamic re-task organizing.

Finally, BCTs need to practice this transition from wide area security to combined arms maneuver and back again. Do it again, and capture lessons learned, not only for the fires warfighting function, but for all six of the warfighting functions.

As General Dempsey alluded to, there is very little to suggest that we will guess correctly as we attempt to deduce the nature of future conflict. We will, no doubt, "get it wrong." Nevertheless, from our in depth analysis of agility and the fires warfighting function, there are some takeaways that will allow us to hedge our bets, that will allow us to manage uncertainty, and most importantly, will enable victory in any potential operational environment. Using the comprehensive working definition of agility, we proposed priorities that future leaders can use to chart a course to General Dempsey's "Pervasive Agility." Agility is about winning, and we can navigate towards future victory by developing training plans that enable agility by focusing on fundamentals across the spectrum of operations, that build agile organizations that are capable of recognizing changing conditions and adapting accordingly, and that practice agility by establishing and enforcing versatile standards and processes.

There is no guarantee that this roadmap will lead to future victory; however, if we choose to ignore the precepts of agility, if we willingly decide to turn our backs on the hard-fought lessons learned from the demonstrated but limited adaptability of our last ten years of operational experience, and if we simplistically return to preparing for conflicts of previous eras, we will almost certainly arrive someplace where we don't want to be.

Pervasive Agility: Owning the Function to Prevent, Shape and Win

"This is a town full of losers, and I'm pulling out of here to win."[44]
--Bruce Springsteen

The Army stands at a historic crossroads, a strategic transition with profound implications for the future of our nation. We've been in similar situations before, and unfortunately, we've botched this transition before. As General Dempsey stated, it's more likely than not that we will be wrong as we look towards the future. But that's not to say that we should not try. Upon assuming his duties as the chairman of the Joint Chiefs of Staff, he acknowledged the challenges in front of us and wrote, "Transitioning out of a constant combat posture to being ready to fight across all domains will require deep thinking—about the capabilities we need and about who we are."[45]

Given the uncertainty of the situation, our national leaders have done some "deep thinking" and provided us with a conceptual roadmap based upon a logical premise—that we will need to be agile and adaptable. Operational adaptability and pervasive agility are good ideas that will prevent us from botching this transition again. We can't simply turn back the clock to the training environment of 2000 and wish away the threats of the contemporary environment. Similarly, it would be foolish to assume that we'll never need the skills and the hard fought lessons learned of the last ten years. General Dempsey continued: "We must develop a Joint Force for 2020 that remains ready to answer the Nation's call—anytime, anywhere. We need to offset fewer resources with more innovation."[46]

Echoing General Dempsey's challenge, General Odierno wrote: "Army leaders accept that there are no predetermined solutions to problems. Army leaders adapt their thinking, formations, and employment techniques to the specific situation they face. This requires an adaptable and innovative mind, a willingness to accept prudent risk in unfamiliar or rapidly changing situations, and an ability to adjust based on continuous assessment."[47]

This paper has attempted to contribute some "deep thinking" to the conversation by exploring the nature of agility within the context of the current strategic environment. First, having identified the strategic imperative of agility in the current strategic debate, we developed a comprehensive definition of agility that blends the positive attributes of the common definition with the evolution of the concept of agility as it has appeared in our capstone operational doctrine. From that, we posited a comprehensive working definition that incorporates the implicit intellectual component of agility and accounts for the attendant benchmark of success. Agility, in our definition, is about recognizing changing circumstances, nimbly and effectively adapting to those circumstances. Ultimately, agility is about winning and victory. Second, we examined agility within the context of our most recent operational experience by focusing on Soldiers, leaders and units of the field artillery and the Fires Warfighting function, determining that although admirable, the "agility" of our COIN campaigns in Iraq and Afghanistan were limited and unidirectional; in short; the agility that our senior leaders are calling for, the "pervasive agility" of the future force, will require a more agile agility. Agility will require Soldiers, leaders, and units that possess the ability to execute operations at both ends of the spectrum, not only the skills and competencies required by the traditional demands of high intensity conflict of combined arms maneuver (CAM), but also the finesse and subtlety of the non-traditional environment of wide area security (WAS). More importantly, agility of the future will require the ability to transition seamlessly between the two core competencies, or execute both simultaneously. Finally, we attempted to translate this abstract concept of agility into a practical roadmap, again, by focusing on the fires warfighting function, in order to offer priorities to leaders as they attempt to achieve agility in the face of competing priorities and limited resources.

The future will require an Army capable of decisive action, forces that are capable of applying a combination of stability and defeat mechanisms across a spectrum of conflict that encompasses combined arms maneuver and wide area security. More importantly, we must be agile and adaptable enough to be capable of one type of combat, or the other, and more likely, both simultaneously. This environment will require what General Dempsey has called pervasive agility, a more agile flexibility and versatility that must permeate the entire organization. This pervasive agility not only provides the roadmap for the future, but it artfully blends the lessons learned from the last ten years of war with our institutional memory of combined arms operations.

This paper has proposed some "deep thinking" on the concept of agility. Thinking is the easy part. Now we need to put that thinking into action.

Now the hard work begins.

Endnotes:

[1] Barack H. Obama, President of the United States, "Remarks by the President at the United States Naval Academy Commencement," May 22, 2009, www.whitehouse.gov/the_press_office/Remarks-by-the-President-at-US-Naval-Academy-Commencement.

[2] Teresa Tritch, "How the Deficit Got This Big," *New York Times*, July 23, 2011, C2.

[3] Barack H. Obama, President of the United States, Preface to *Sustaining U.S. Global Leadership: Priorities for 21st Century Defense* (Washington DC: Department of Defense, 3 January 2012) 1.

[4] GEN Martin E. Dempsey, Chairman of the US Joint Chiefs of Staff, Foreword in *The Army Capstone Concept, Operational Adaptability: Operating Under Conditions of Uncertainty and Complexity in an Era of Persistent Conflict, 2016-2028,* TRADOC Pamphlet 525-3-0, (Fort Monroe, VA: Training and Doctrine Command, December 21, 2009), i.

[5] Barack H. Obama, President of United States, Preface to *Sustaining U.S. Global Leadership: Priorities for 21st Century Defense* (Washington DC: Department of Defense, 3 January 2012) 1.

[6] Leon Panetta, US Secretary of Defense, Foreword to the *Sustaining U.S. Global Leadership: Priorities for 21st Century Defense* (Washington DC: Department of Defense, 3 January 2012) 3.

[7] Mark Viera, "Coaches Say Knicks Have Found Someone Special," *New York Times*, 9 February 2012, D12.

[8] Walt Whitman, "Song of Myself," *The Norton Anthology of American Literature*, 4th edition, vol. 1 (New York: WW Norton and Co, 1994) 2089.

[9] Frederick C. Mish, editor in chief, *Merriam Webster Collegiate Dictionary, 10th Ed.* (Springfield, MA: Merriam Webster Inc, 1994) 23.

[10] David S. Alberts, Director of Research, Office of the Assistant Secretary of Defense, Network Information and Integration, *The Agility Advantage: A Survival Guide for Complex Enterprises and Endeavors,* (Washington DC: DoD Command and Control Research Program, September 2011) 187-8.

[11] John A. Nagl, *Learning to Eat Soup With a Knife: Counterinsurgency Lessons from Malaya and Vietnam*, (Chicago, IL: University of Chicago Press, 2005) 7.

[12] Headquarters, Department of the Army, Field Manual 3-0, *Operations* (Washington, DC: GPO, 2001) 1-45.

[13] Amos A. Jordan; William J. Taylor, Jr; Michael J. Meese, and Suzanne C. Nielsen, American National Security, 6th Ed. (Baltimore, MD: John Hopkins University Press, 2009) 53.

[14] US Department of the Army, Field Manual 100-5, *Operations* (Washington, DC: GPO, 1 July 1976) 1-1.

[15] John A. Nagl, *Learning to Eat Soup With a Knife: Counterinsurgency Lessons from Malaya and Vietnam*, (Chicago, IL: University of Chicago Press, 2005) 9.

[16] US Department of the Army, TRADOC History—Frequently asked questions (accessed at http://www.tradoc.army.mil/HISTORIAN/faqs.htm; 13 March 2012).

[17] US Department of the Army, TRADOC History—Frequently asked questions (accessed at http://www.tradoc.army.mil/HISTORIAN/faqs.htm; 13 March 2012).

[18] US Department of the Army, Field Manual 100-5, *Operations* (Washington DC: GPO, 14 June 1993) 2-6.

[19] US Department of the Army, Field Manual 100-5, *Operations* (Washington DC: GPO, 14 June 1993) 2-7.

[20] David S. Alberts, Director of Research, Office of the Assistant Secretary of Defense, Network Information and Integration, *The Agility Advantage: A Survival Guide for Complex Enterprises and Endeavors,* (Washington DC: DoD Command and Control Research Program, September 2011) 197.

[21] David S. Alberts, Director of Research, Office of the Assistant Secretary of Defense, Network Information and Integration, *The Agility Advantage: A Survival Guide for Complex Enterprises and Endeavors,* (Washington DC: DoD Command and Control Research Program, September 2011) 190.

[22] David S. Alberts, Director of Research, Office of the Assistant Secretary of Defense, Network Information and Integration, *The Agility Advantage: A Survival Guide for Complex Enterprises and Endeavors,* (Washington DC: DoD Command and Control Research Program, September 2011) 204.

[23] M. F. Ashley Montagu, editor, *Toynbee and History: Critical Essays and Reviews.* (Boston, MA: Porter Sargent, 1956) vi.

[24] "Jim E. Mora," *Wikipedia* (accessed at http://en.wikipedia.org/wiki/Jim_E._Mora; 10 March 2012).

[25] Leon Panetta, US Secretary of Defense, "Willing to Make That Fight; An Address to the AUSA Annual Meeting," *Army*, December 2011, 37.

[26] U.S. Department of the Army, *The Army Capstone Concept; Operational Adaptability: Operating Under Conditions of Uncertainty and Complexity in an Era of Persistent Conflict, 2016-2028,* (TRADOC Pamphlet 525-3-0, (Fort Monroe, VA: Training and Doctrine Command, December 21, 2009) 12.

[27] GEN Robert W. Cone, Commanding General U.S. Army Training and Doctrine Command, "Laying the Groundwork for the Army of 2020," (Arlington, VA: Association of the U.S. Army Institute for Land Warfare, Landpower Essay No 11-2, August 2011), 2.

[28] U.S. Department of the Army, *Unified Land Operations, Army Doctrinal Publication 3-0,* (Washington D.C.: GPO, 10 October 2011) 14.

[29] Robert O. Babcock, *Operation Iraqi Freedom I, A Year in the Sunni Triangle: The History of the 4th Infantry Division and Task Force Ironhorse in Iraq, April 2003 to April 2004,* (Tuscaloosa, AL: St. John's Press, 2005) 297.

[30] Dr. Donald P. Wright, Colonel Timothy R. Reese, with the Contemporary Operations Study Team, *On Point II, Transition to the New Campaign*, (Fort Leavenworth, KS: Combat Studies Institute Press, 2008) 36.

[31] GEN Raymond T. Odierno, "Division Operations Across the Spectrum—Combat to SOSO in Iraq" interview by Patrecia Slayden Hollis, *Field Artillery Journal*, March-June 2004. 11.

[32] GEN Martin E. Dempsey, Chairman of the US Joint Chiefs of Staff, "Win, Learn, Focus, Adapt, Win Again," *Army Magazine*, March 2011. 25.

[33] U.S. Department of the Army, *Unified Land Operations*, Army Doctrine Publication 3-0 (Washington, DC: US Department of the Army, October 2011) 6, and US Department of the Army, *The Army Operating Concept*, TRADOC Pamphlet 525-3-1, (Fort Monroe, VA: Training and Doctrine Command, 19 August 2010), 11.

[34] GEN Raymond T. Odierno, Chief of Staff of the US Army, " Marching Orders, America's Force of Decisive Action," (Washington D.C.: Headquarters, US Army, January 2012), 5.

[35] GEN Martin E. Dempsey, Chairman of the US Joint Chiefs of Staff, Foreword in *The Army Capstone Concept, Operational Adaptability: Operating Under Conditions of Uncertainty and Complexity in an Era of Persistent Conflict, 2016-2028*, TRADOC Pamphlet 525-3-0, (Fort Monroe, VA: Training and Doctrine Command, December 21, 2009), i.

[36] GEN Robert W. Cone, Commanding General U.S. Army Training and Doctrine Command, "Laying the Groundwork for the Army of 2020," (Arlington, VA: Association of the U.S. Army Institute for Land Warfare, Landpower Essay No 11-2, August 2011), 2.

[37] Jim Garamone, "Dempsey Details Vision of 2020 Military Strategy," Armed Forces Press Service, www/defense.gov/news article/Dempsey_2020 vision/web.archive.

[38] Leo Tolstoy, *War and Peace*, translated by Richard Pevear and Larissa Volokhonsky (New York, NY: Alfred Knopf, 2007) 1028.

[39] Robert Frost, "The Road Not Taken,*" Frost: Collected Poems, Prose, and Plays* (New York, NY: Library of America, 1995) 103.

[40] David S. Alberts, Director of Research, Office of the Assistant Secretary of Defense, Network Information and Integration, *The Agility Advantage: A Survival Guide for Complex Enterprises and Endeavors,* (Washington DC: DoD Command and Control Research Program, September 2011) 3.

[41] GEN Martin Dempsey, speech at the George C. Marshall Army ROTC Award Seminar, Lexington, Va. April 17, 2009, (accessed at http://www.tradoc.army.mil/pao/Speeches/GenDempsey20200809/MarshallROTCAward.html).

[42] BG Thomas S. Vandal, Commandant of the Field Artillery School, "Growing a New Field Artillery," *Fires Journal*, September-October 2011, 4.

[43]U.S. Department of the Army, *The Army Operating Concept, 2016-2028*, (TRADOC Pamphlet 525-3-1, (Fort Monroe, VA: Training and Doctrine Command, December 21, 2009) 27.

[44] Bruce Springsteen, *Songs*, (New York, NY: Avon Books, 1998), 49.

[45] GEN Martin E. Dempsey, Chairman of the US Joint Chiefs of Staff, Foreword in the *Chairman's Strategic Direction for the Joint Force,* (Washington, D.C.: GPO, February 2012) 2.

[46] GEN Martin E. Dempsey, Chairman of the US Joint Chiefs of Staff, Foreword in the *Chairman's Strategic Direction for the Joint Force,* (Washington, D.C.: GPO, February 2012) 2.

[47] GEN Raymond T. Odierno, Chief of Staff of the US Army, "Marching Orders, America's Force of Decisive Action," (Washington D.C.: Headquarters, US Army, January 2012), 4.